W9-CLV-424

COPING WITH
ILLNESS

Liz Miles

Heinemann
LIBRARY

Chicago, Illinois

www.heinemannraintree.com
Visit our website to find out more information about Heinemann-Raintree books.

To order:
☎ Phone 888-454-2279
🖥 Visit www.heinemannraintree.com to browse our catalog and order online.

Edited by Louise Galpine and Laura Knowles
Designed by Richard Parker
Original illustrations © Capstone Global Library
    Ltd 2011
Picture research by Liz Alexander

Originated by Capstone Global Library Ltd
Printed and bound in the United States of America,
    North Mankato, MN

15 14 13 12 11
10 9 8 7 6 5 4 3 2 1

Library of Congress Cataloging-in-Publication Data
Miles, Liz.
  Coping with illness / Liz Miles.
    p. cm. — (Real life issues)
  Includes bibliographical references and index.
  ISBN 978-1-4329-4763-7 (hc)
  1. Diseases—Juvenile literature. 2. Children—
Diseases—Juvenile literature. I. Title.
  R130.5.M52 2011
  616—dc22
  2010021047

Acknowledgments
The author and publisher are grateful to the following for permission to reproduce copyright material: © CCA p. 30; Alamy pp. 9 (© Paul Doyle), 13 (© Lisa F. Young), 43 (© PhotoAlto), 34 (© Spencer Grant); Corbis pp. 6 (© Dr. Gopal Murti/Visuals Unlimited), 21 (© FEDERICO GAMBARINI/epa), 26 (© Peter Turnley), 28 (© Beau Lark), 35 (© Image Source); Getty Images pp. 7 (Colin Hawkins/Cultura), 10 (Elliot Elliot/Johner Images), 15 (Brent Stirton/Getty Images for the GBC), 27 (Jose Luis Pelaez Inc/Blend Images); Photolibrary pp. 8 (Image Source), 12 (Corbis), 16 (Denis Meyer/imagebroker.net), 20 (ERproductions Ltd/Blend Images), 24 (Juice Images), 37 (Comstock), 19, 23; Press Association Images p. 41 (Fiona Hanson/PA Wire/PA Archive); Science Photo Library pp. 17 (Paul Rapson), 33 (Coneyl Jay), Shutterstock pp. 5 (© Monkey Business Images), 39 (© maga).

"Distressed texture" design detail reproduced with permission of iStockphoto/© Diana Walters.

Cover photograph of a worried boy lying on a bed reproduced with permission of Photolibrary/Image Source.

Quotation on page 14 extracted from Surya Bhattacharya, "Orphans of AIDS: Missing Out on Your Childhood," *Faze Magazine* (Issue 20), www.fazemagazine.com. Quotation on page 17 reproduced by permission of Connect with Kids. For information, visit www.connectwithkids.com.

We would like to thank Anne Pezalla for her invaluable help in the preparation of this book.

Every effort has been made to contact copyright holders of material reproduced in this book. Any omissions will be rectified in subsequent printings if notice is given to the publishers.

In order to protect the privacy of individuals, some names in this book have been changed.

CONTENTS

⚠️

Stay safe on the Internet!
When you are on the Internet, never give personal details such as
your real name, phone number, or address to anyone you have
only had contact with online. If you are contacted by anyone
who makes you feel uncomfortable or upset, don't reply, tell an
adult, and block that person from contacting you again.

Any words appearing in the text in bold, **like this**, are
explained in the glossary.

Introduction

Most of us have felt unwell at some time. Perhaps you have had a bad cold, or something more serious. Illness is part of our lives, and it is important to know how to cope with it.

Every illness is different

Many illnesses, such as a sore throat, pass quickly without treatment. Other illnesses, such as **cancer**, are serious and need treatment. Some illnesses are there from birth, while others are caught as infections or appear for complicated reasons. Any part of the body can become ill, from ears to stomachs. Many illnesses are invisible to us, such as **disorders** of the brain.

Caregivers

Caregivers look after people who are sick and help them to cope. Some are specially trained, but many caregivers are simply the partner, parent, child, or other relative of the patient. They have to learn a lot about the patient's needs, and they must also know when to ask for help.

Coping

Whether it is you or someone you know who is sick, coping during these times can be difficult. This book suggests ways to cope. It is important to ask for help when you need it. There are many well-trained people who can provide support. You can find organizations that can help you on pages 46–47.

Some hospitals are specifically for children and young adults. The people who work there enjoy helping young patients.

Online!

There is a huge amount of information about illnesses on the Internet. However, every illness affects people differently. If you are sick, it is best to ask your doctor any questions. Remember that information on the Internet can be inaccurate. Have an adult help you figure out which websites are reliable.

What Is Illness?

Illnesses range from mild to serious. Mild illnesses usually come and go and are not difficult to cope with. Other illnesses have to be treated by trained people, such as doctors.

Common cold

The common cold is the illness that affects us most. On average, children catch 6 to 10 colds a year. The symptoms can include coughing, a runny nose, and a headache. There are over 200 **viruses** that can cause a cold. A healthy body can fight a cold virus, making the cold usually disappear after 7 to 10 days. Although the symptoms are uncomfortable, a cold is not difficult to cope with. A bad cold might make you want to stay in bed. Some people take medicines such as painkillers to help them feel more comfortable.

This is what the common cold virus looks like through a microscope.

Staying at home

If you are feeling sick, it can sometimes be best to stay at home. If there is a chance that you could make other people sick, you should stay at home until you feel better. This will help reduce the chance of you passing your illness on to others.

If you have a cold, always sneeze into a tissue and put the tissue in the garbage. Other people are then less likely to catch your cold.

CASE STUDY

Oliver, age 9, remembers having a bad cold and feeling too sick to go to school and needing to rest. "I stayed at home and kept warm. I could not do anything, so I lay on the sofa. I even had to turn off the television since the flashing colors made my head feel weird."

Long-term illnesses

Some illnesses are **long-term** and can even last a lifetime.
Long-term illnesses include **asthma** and **autism**. Understanding
a long-term illness is the first step in coping—whether you are the
sufferer or the friend or relative of a sufferer.

Asthmatic friend

Asthma sufferers may need to inhale a medicine to help them
breathe. To be an understanding friend, make sure you give
friends with asthma the space and time to use their inhalers.

Give a child space when
she or he uses an inhaler.

Understanding autism

Children with autism can have problems communicating and fitting in. They might find it hard to see other people's points of view. An autistic child might:

- not look you in the eyes
- not want to play with other children
- get upset by loud noise and cover his or her ears.

Before **diagnosis**, people sometimes wrongly think autistic children are misbehaving because they do not follow instructions and can get upset easily. Scientists think that children with autism have slightly different brain structures than non-autistic children.

Autism is described as an "invisible disability" because you cannot always tell if people have it when you meet them.

CASE STUDY

Understanding what it means to be autistic can make you more sensitive and caring toward those with autism. Charlie, age 9, has a brother, age 7, who is autistic. Charlie describes his brother like this: "He doesn't like being touched. He wants to dress the same as me. I have to keep an eye on him on the street to make sure he's safe. At school, he has a teaching assistant to help him. Sometimes people ask him if he wants to play but he doesn't want to join in. Sometimes when he's angry he hits himself on the head. He can be a bit annoying, like when he likes touching people's loose teeth or mosquito bites."

Life-threatening illnesses

Some illnesses are very serious and need urgent treatment. Life-threatening illnesses can bring an end to a patient's life. However, if a patient receives treatment, he or she can cope and live for many years. For example, a patient who has a major **heart attack** might have an operation on his or her heart. Without the operation, the patient could die. After the operation, the patient will probably be able to live a fairly normal life.

Terminal illness

Some illnesses are so serious that they are described as terminal. Sadly, this means that the patient will die. Doctors can rarely predict how long it will take for a patient to die from a terminal illness. A dying person needs lots of care.

If you know someone who is dying, it is important to talk about your feelings. Many people are afraid of death because they don't know what it will feel like. Other people may not feel sad about dying at all. They may have led a happy life and are content with the idea of dying.

People who are very sick usually love to have visitors.

BEHIND THE HEADLINES

Scientists are always searching for ways to cure illnesses. Recently, scientists have begun to make new organs using a patient's own **stem cells**. In 2009 a 10-year-old boy was given a new trachea, or windpipe (see below), created from his own stem cells. The trachea he was born with was too narrow for him to breathe. With the new trachea, the boy was able to breathe normally.

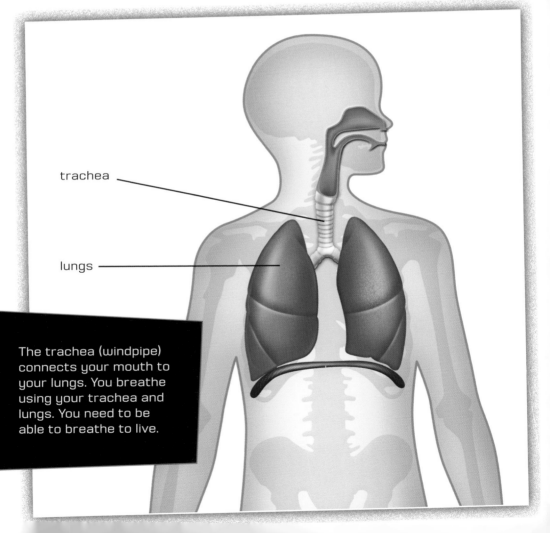

trachea

lungs

The trachea (windpipe) connects your mouth to your lungs. You breathe using your trachea and lungs. You need to be able to breathe to live.

Who Is Affected?

Anyone can be affected by illness, and a person can become sick at any time in his or her life. However, some people are more vulnerable (likely to develop an illness) than others. This group includes babies and older people.

Babies

Some babies are born with an illness or condition. Often it is not serious, and the baby will be kept in the hospital for just a few days. If it is more serious, the baby may be put in an incubator. This is a closed-in cot that keeps the baby warm and helps him or her to breathe. It can be a worrying time for parents, brothers, and sisters.

An incubator is sealed to protect the baby from germs.

Older people

Older people often suffer from illnesses. As bodies age, they become frail and parts wear out. Older people may need more care and help at home. Families often try to help the oldest members of their family.

Arthritis is the common name for conditions that make the joints and bones painful. In older people, a wearing away in the joints can make walking painful. If it is serious, they may go to the hospital for an operation. The surgeon puts in a replacement hip or knee joint.

Older people sometimes need help with everyday tasks.

BEHIND THE HEADLINES

Many people were frightened when a new type of flu spread around the world in 2009. It was called swine flu because it was thought to have started in pigs. Most people who catch it get better after a few days. However, vulnerable people, such as children under 5, adults over 65, and people suffering from certain illnesses, can die from swine flu. Many countries quickly tried to get their most vulnerable people **vaccinated**.

Caring for a parent

Illness also affects the people who live with or know the patient. Some children have to take care of their parents. Thousands of children under 18 years old help to care for a parent or other relative at home. Many get help from professionals, such as nurses, but in some cases there is no other adult at home to help. Children as young as five help to care for people with physical and mental disabilities. See the website of the American Association of Caregiving Youth on page 47. This groups offers help ranging from ideas on how to keep up-to-date with your homework to places to contact to get extra help at home.

Orphans in Africa

A disease known as **AIDS** is a serious problem in some African countries. AIDS is caused by a **virus** called HIV. This virus has spread rapidly across Africa because many countries are too poor to provide health education to teach people how to protect themselves against it. The lack of money means that medicines are in short supply, too. In South Africa alone, 1.4 million children have become orphans because of AIDS. The illness caused the deaths of their mothers and fathers. Older relatives often take care of the children.

CASE STUDY

An article by Faze Magazine tells the story of 13-year-old Patience, who lives in a village in Zimbabwe. "Patience lost her mom six years ago, and her dad abandoned the family when Patience's mom first got sick … Two years ago, when her aunt was unable to feed her, Patience started living on her own, surviving on support from a local community group … She is able to afford only two meals a day." There are many organizations you can support to help children like Patience cope.

It is often hard for grandparents of AIDS orphans to find the extra money to buy food for their grandchildren.

Finding Out What Is Wrong

If you feel unwell, in pain, or as though something is wrong with a part of your body, it is important to tell your parents. They may take you to a doctor, who will usually be able to figure out what the problem is. If the doctor is unsure, he or she might suggest some tests.

Simple tests

Most tests are simple, quick, and don't hurt at all. Sometimes a sample of your blood is sent to a **laboratory**, and the results come back in a few days. Blood samples can tell the doctor if your organs and glands are working properly.

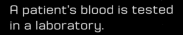

A patient's blood is tested in a laboratory.

BEHIND THE HEADLINES

It has been reported that 4 to 8 percent of children are affected by food allergies, and the numbers are increasing. An allergy is when the body reacts to a normal food type as if it is harmful. Symptoms include dizziness, vomiting, and rashes. Tests find out which foods the child is allergic to, so that they can be avoided. Only eight foods cause 90 percent of food allergies. They are cow's milk, eggs, peanuts, nuts from trees (such as walnuts), fish, shellfish, soybeans, and wheat.

A scratch test will show which food a person is allergic to.

CASE STUDY

It is important to know what to avoid if you have a serious allergy. Some people suffer from life-threatening symptoms, such as not being able to breathe. Jeff, age 10, is allergic to peanuts, and even the smell of them sets off a reaction. Jeff says: "My throat swells up and my lips swell too and I have trouble breathing."

Hospital tests

Some tests are done in hospitals or doctors' offices, using special equipment. These tests include the use of heart monitors to check that the heart is beating correctly and **X-ray** machines that show images of bones and organs inside the body.

Scans

A CT scanner is a special X-ray machine that gives very detailed images of parts inside the body, such as the brain. A person lies in a CT scanner while rays are aimed at his or her body. The person has to keep very still, but it does not hurt.

Biopsies

A **biopsy** is carried out in hospitals and doctors' offices. Sometimes lumps appear in women's breasts or other parts of the body. These need to be checked to make sure they are not **cancerous**. A sample of the lump is taken and sent to a laboratory. If the result shows the lump is **benign** (not **cancer**), everyone is relieved. If it is **malignant**, that means the lump is cancerous and has to be removed.

CASE STUDY

Anna's stepmother found a lump on her breast. The lump was removed and tested. Anna, her stepmom, and her dad were worried about what the results would be, but the doctor explained that most lumps (80 percent) are benign. Even if the lump was malignant, most women are free of breast cancer for the rest of their lives after treatment, especially if the lump is found and treated soon after it appears. A few days later they got the result: benign. It was a relief for the whole family.

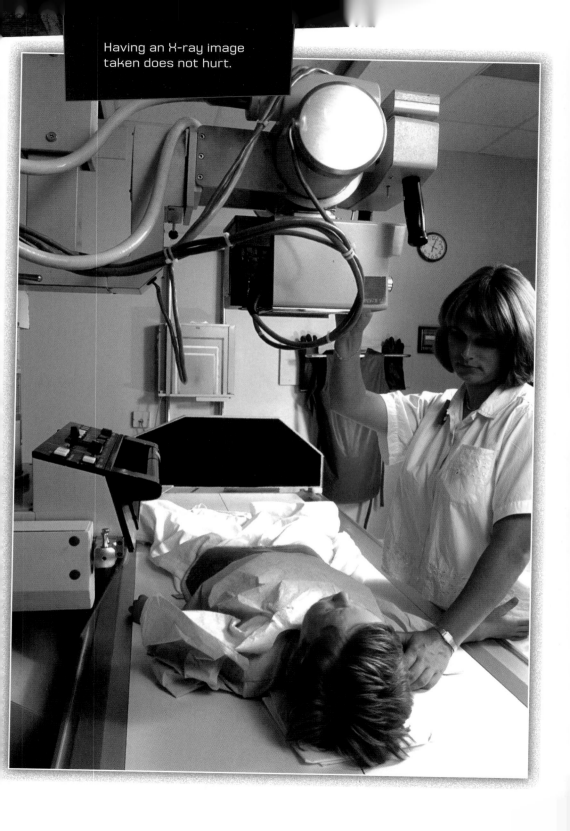

Having an X-ray image taken does not hurt.

Going to the Hospital

Most people first go to a doctor if they are sick. The doctor asks questions, examines the patient, and carries out simple tests. Doctors will often listen to your heart and use equipment to examine your eyes, nose, or throat.

Sometimes it is necessary for a person to go to the hospital. A visit can be for just a few hours, or longer with overnight stays. People go to hospital for all kinds of reasons. Here are a few:

- emergency care, such as after an accident
- further tests to find out what is wrong
- an operation, or surgery
- special medical treatment, such as **chemotherapy**
- **counseling**.

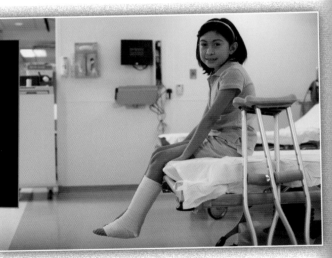

Urgent treatment is available in emergency rooms at hospitals.

Emergency rooms

If you have an accident, you will be taken to the emergency room. A relative might take you in a car, or an ambulance might take you. The doctors and nurses treat the most seriously sick or injured patients first. They will be kind and caring.

Hospitals around the world

Hospitals in many countries, such as the United States, United Kingdom, and Australia, are usually comfortable, clean, and have good equipment. Unfortunately, hospitals can be quite different in poorer countries, and especially after a natural disaster, such as an earthquake.

BEHIND THE HEADLINES

On January 12, 2010, an earthquake destroyed buildings and killed and injured many people in Haiti, a country in the Caribbean. Hospitals were soon overcrowded. Many people, including children and babies, had to lie on the floor or outside on the ground. There were not enough doctors or equipment.

After an earthquake in Haiti in 2010, the hospitals were overcrowded. This meant that many patients had to be treated outside.

Staying overnight

You may have to stay overnight in a hospital. It might seem scary at first because it is different from what you are used to, but you will soon feel happier and comfortable. The friendly doctors and nurses will take care of you. Hospitals have special areas just for children. These parts of hospitals are usually colorful, with plenty of books and games and a television so you do not get bored.

CASE STUDY

Suna, age 9, remembers the best things about her stay in the hospital: a television with movies, a playroom, delicious food, and two kind nurses.

The people you meet

Going to the hospital is serious, but there are ways to make it fun. You will meet other children who are sick. Some will be well enough to talk or to play; others will not. You will also meet people who do interesting jobs. Some of these are:

- nurses: They work with doctors and make sure your stay is comfortable.
- specialists: These doctors know a great deal about certain illnesses.
- surgeons: These doctors perform operations.

Online!

You can find out what it is like to stay in a hospital by looking at children's hospital websites on the Internet. The Kids' Health website (see page 46) also has a section that lets you know what you can expect during your stay.

Some children have to stay in the hospital for a long time. There is plenty for them to do, such as playing games, painting, and drawing. Some kids do their schoolwork if they feel well enough.

Operations

You may have to go to the hospital for an operation. Some people are frightened, but the nurses and doctors will make sure you are comfortable. Your parents will be able to stay with you most of the time.

In a hospital, everyone will try hard to keep you cheerful, but feeling scared is perfectly normal.

Feeling numb

For most operations you will have a general anesthetic, which stops you from feeling any pain and makes you go to sleep. For some treatments, such as having a bad cut stitched up, you will have a local anesthetic. This numbs only a part of the body, so you are still awake while you are being treated.

Before ...

You may go to a pre-op appointment before an operation. The doctors and nurses will tell you all about what is going to happen, and you can ask any questions you like. If you are having a general anesthetic, you will not be allowed to eat for a few hours before the operation. Before being taken to the operating room, you might be given a premedication. This will stop you from feeling worried or scared.

... and after

After it is all over you will wake up in a recovery room, where the nurses will keep a close eye on you. You will feel tired, perhaps a little sick, and sore. Soon you will be taken back to your room, where you can rest until you feel well again.

CASE STUDY

George, age 8, went into the hospital for an ear operation. He said, "I saw a nurse before the operation who told me what would happen.... My mommy came to the operating room with me and was in the recovery room when I woke up. I had bandages over my ears, so did my teddy bear. I felt a bit sick but soon felt fine." Overall, George said, "It was a good experience, but going home was my favorite part!"

Prevention and Treatment

We need to take care of our bodies to help prevent illness. For example, we should eat the right foods, in the right amounts.

Every day in the world, 16,000 children die from hunger-related illnesses. People in poorer countries, such as Somalia, often suffer from **starvation** (lack of food) when there is no food available. In richer countries, **obesity** is a problem because of high-fat foods and because many people do not get enough exercise. In the United States, a survey showed that 17 percent of children ages 2 to 19 years are obese. Obesity can eventually lead to life-threatening illnesses, such as high blood pressure and diabetes.

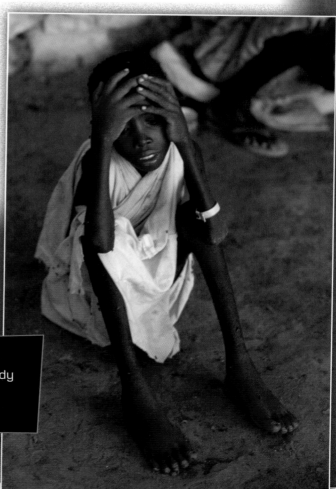

Starvation stops the body from working properly.

What causes obesity?

Obesity is not always caused by overeating or eating the wrong sorts of food. It can be caused by things such as stress, genetics (qualities that are passed down by your parents), and a low **metabolism**. If you are overweight, it is probably a good idea to lose weight. But before you try, you must ask a doctor how to lose weight safely.

Unfortunately, obese children and adults are sometimes bullied. This makes things far worse. Bullying should never happen, so if you or someone you know is being bullied, tell a parent or teacher.

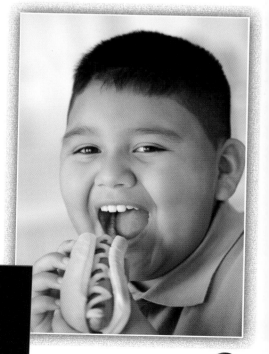

Eating the wrong kind of foods can lead to obesity and life-threatening illnesses.

You can help care for a sick relative in all kinds of ways.

Talking

When people are sick, they often have to be cared for at home by relatives or friends. **Long-term** illnesses can mean many years of hard work. If you have a relative at home who is seriously ill, you will feel all kinds of emotions. You might feel upset, worried, or even angry. It is important to talk to people about how you feel. Find someone you can trust at home or at school. Remember that usually illness is not anyone's fault.

Hospital care

Some accidents can leave people severely **disabled**. For example, brain damage can change their lives forever. The patient may never be able to go home from the hospital. If you have a relative who is in the hospital long-term, you will probably visit him or her. To make the most of your visits, plan them in advance. Think of interesting, happy things to say. Take something to show, such as photographs.

Online!

Seventeen-year-old Sophie Wilkinson was in a tragic car accident. Her brain was so badly damaged that she has been in a **vegetative state** ever since. She needs full-time care from hospitals and her family. You can visit the Sophie's Gift website (www.sophies-gift.org) to find out how her family cares for Sophie and how they are thanking Sophie's hospital.

Treatments

It helps to remember that many new treatments are becoming available, including new drugs and technology. New treatments mean that people are surviving with diseases that they would have died from not long ago.

Five-year-old Eli Walker suffers from a type of cancer called leukemia. In 2009 he was named a Community Hero by the Children's Cancer Association for his courage in battling the disease.

Kicking cancer

Cancer is a disease in which cells (the tiny things that make up the body) grow and divide too much and can start to destroy the body. There are more than 200 different types of cancer. Cancer treatments are often successful today. With the right treatment, most patients can beat cancer.

CASE STUDY

Judy was told she had a type of cancer known as Hodgkin's disease when she was 14 years old, and had never heard of the illness before. She was very, very sick. After a month of tests, she had 12 **chemotherapy** treatments. Her hair fell out (but later grew back). She missed a lot of school. But eight months after she first became sick, she had an **X-ray**. She was thrilled to be told that the cancer was gone. Judy is now in her thirties and cancer free, and she has three children of her own.

Online!

Research into curing diseases, such as cancer, is important. Many organizations are involved in raising money for research and offering support to patients. Even if you don't know someone who has had cancer, you might like to get involved in raising money for a charity. Look for fundraising events on the Internet, such as at the Children's Cancer Association or the American Cancer Society websites.

Fears and Worries

We all like to fit in and be accepted by our friends. It can be difficult if we become sick, because it makes us feel different. It is important to talk about any worries you might have. Talking helps you figure things out and lets other people help you.

CASE STUDY

Judy (see page 31) wants sick children to learn from her experience and to be open about how they feel. She wishes she had talked more to family and friends when she was sick. She wishes she had told them she was afraid.

Being normal

Some illnesses force people to do things that others do not have to do. Thousands of children suffer from type 1 diabetes. People with this illness have problems with their pancreas, an organ in their body. Their pancreas does not make enough **insulin**. This means they are unable to make use of glucose (sugar) from food. People with type 1 diabetes have to inject insulin into their bodies to do the job. They also have to eat healthy meals at planned times and check their sugar levels.

If you have type 1 diabetes, it is important to explain the illness to your friends. A teacher or parent will help you. Once people know, you will not feel so embarrassed or different.

Online!

If you have diabetes, ask a parent to look for diabetes **support groups** on the Internet (see page 47 for a website address). Talking to other children with diabetes can help with any worries or fears. You will get tips on how to cope with the illness and how to explain it to people.

Some people with diabetes have to inject themselves with insulin, but they soon get used to it.

Mental health

Mental health problems and **disorders** cause all kinds of fears and worries. You may know someone who behaves in an unusual way, which can sometimes be frightening. But if you learn about the person's problem or disorder, your fears will probably change into sympathy and understanding.

ADHD

Attention-deficit hyperactivity disorder (called ADHD) is one of the most common chronic (ongoing) conditions suffered by children. In the United States, just over 8 percent of children ages 6 to 17 have been **diagnosed** with the condition. ADHD makes it difficult for children to control how they behave, sit still, pay attention, or concentrate. ADHD is not anyone's fault.

The more a teacher knows about ADHD, the better he or she will be able to support students with the condition.

Help

If you have ADHD, you may be given medicine, taught how to relax, or go to see a therapist. A therapist will help you plan tactics to make life easier. If you know children with this problem, try to help them. Never be cruel or call them names.

If you know people in school who have ADHD, don't distract them during work time. This will make it easier for them to concentrate.

Online!

If you have ADHD, you are not alone. Try reading other people's stories. You might pick up some tips on how to cope. Telling your own story can help, too. Writing everything down makes things clearer and less scary. Keeping a journal or posting your feelings and experiences online can really help. You can both read and share at the ADDitude website (see page 47 for details).

Talking It Over

Many children suffer from anxiety or sadness, but these feelings are usually not connected with mental illness. However, children who do suffer from a **mental disorder** should get professional support and help. Talking about the problem is the first step to feeling better.

Whether you have a mental disorder not, if you are sad or upset, angry, or frightened, it is important to talk about your feelings to people you trust. Talk to a relative, teacher, doctor, or other trusted adult.

Organizations

Around the world there are organizations created to help people deal with specific diseases and problems. These organizations often have helpful websites that are full of other people's stories and experiences. Reading other people's stories can help you realize you are not alone. You can find many of these organizations on the Internet (see pages 46–47).

Express yourself!

Expressing your feelings is important. Talking to people is one way to do this. Perhaps painting a picture can be a way of expressing your feelings, too. If you are angry, play a sport, or even shout into a pillow.

Mental health problems can be treated with support, **counseling**, and sometimes medicine. Talking openly about these problems is important.

Eating disorders

People with severe eating **disorders**, such as **bulimia** and **anorexia**, may not realize they have these illnesses. This means it is very important to support sufferers. If you think you suffer from an eating disorder, it is important to tell someone you trust.

Warning signs

It is sometimes hard to know for certain if you, or someone you know, has an eating disorder. Early signs include:

- a major change in eating habits, such as not eating the food on a plate
- thinking your body or parts of it are large when they aren't
- an obvious loss of weight or obvious changes in weight.

If you notice some of these signs in a friend, ask an adult for advice about what to do.

CASE STUDY

If you know someone who has an eating disorder, you can use the Internet to find ways to help. At the National Eating Disorders Association website (see page 47), you can read about how to support a sufferer. Ideas include:
- Share your concerns, mentioning specific instances when you noticed a problem with the person's eating habits.
- Recommend that the person get help, and maybe even help him or her find an expert to talk to.
- Avoid blaming the person or trying to make him or her feel guilty.
- Let the person know you will always be there for support. With help and support, people with eating disorders can get better again.

Struggling with an eating disorder is hard. If you know someone who is affected by anorexia or bulimia, try to be sensitive and supportive.

Coping Together

Coping with the illness of yourself or others can feel scary and unfair. However, illness can also help to bring people together. Everyone becomes sick at some point in his or her life. People are eager to support and help each other when they feel unwell.

Caring for others

The best way to cope with someone's illness is to find out about the illness. You will then be better able to understand how the person is feeling. Being caring and thoughtful will help the person to feel better. If you feel upset, talk to someone. You must take care of yourself as well as others!

Caring for yourself

If you are sick, it is important to ask for help. Friends, family, and professionals will be happy to offer advice. If you would rather ask for help or advice from somebody who doesn't know you, contact experts from an organization specializing in the disease or condition that affects you (see pages 46–47).

If you go to see a doctor, or go to the hospital, it is important to do what the doctors and nurses suggest. Everything they say and ask you to do is because they want you to get better.

BEHIND THE HEADLINES

In 2006 the lives of six-year-old Mollie and her four-year-old brother, Cameron, suddenly changed. Their mother, Wendy, was **diagnosed** with **cancer**. The children wanted to take care of her so that their dad, David, could continue working. Every day they had to wash, dress, and make breakfast for their mom. In 2009 Mollie and Cameron were given a Children of Courage award for caring for their sick mother and for coping so well.

Mollie and Cameron Millard cared for their mother when she was sick with cancer.

Top Ten Tips for Coping with Illness

If you or others around you are facing illness, you might feel helpless. Here is a list of things to remember to help you cope and beat the illness:

1. Find out about the illness. Don't be afraid to ask questions. Doctors are the best sources of information.

2. Don't be afraid to talk about how you feel. Everyone feels different emotions at different times. It is better to talk about them with someone you trust and not bottle them up.

3. Share your experiences with people who are going through the same sort of thing. There are **support groups** for most illnesses and support groups for caregivers.

4. Follow instructions from doctors and nurses if you are unwell. They are trying to help you, so it is polite to be helpful, too.

5. Be sensitive toward people who are sick. Don't ask them questions or mention the illness unless you are sure they want you to.

6. If you are sick, remember that your family and friends will be worried about you. Sometimes they will show that they are worried, but sometimes they will hide it.

7. Don't talk about a person's illness without thinking first. Remember that some things are private. If you want to pass on personal information, ask permission first.

8. If someone is sick, try to be positive. If the person becomes angry or upset, remember that it is not your fault. The person will be going through all sorts of emotions.

9. Remember that illness isn't anyone's fault. Nobody can be blamed for getting sick or making someone sick.

10. Keeping a diary is a good way to cope with illness. If you are sick, or you know someone who is, write down how you feel and what happens.

If you are sick, talking about how you feel can help.

Glossary

AIDS serious condition that is caused by a virus called HIV

anorexia (anorexia nervosa) mental health condition that makes a person want to avoid eating

asthma disease that affects the tubes that carry air to and from the lungs and makes breathing difficult

Attention-deficit hyperactivity disorder (ADHD) condition that makes it difficult for people to control how they behave, sit still, pay attention, or concentrate

autism condition in which people have problems communicating and fitting in. They might find it hard to see other people's points of view.

benign type of growth that has no signs of cancer

biopsy removal of tissue (cells) under the skin that is then tested

bulimia (bulimia nervosa) mental health condition that causes a person to overeat and then vomit (throw up)

cancer disease in which abnormal cells grow in the body

cancerous linked to the disease cancer

chemotherapy special drugs that are used to treat diseases such as cancer

counseling meeting with a trained person who can talk through problems with you, giving you information and advice

diagnosis figuring out what disease a patient has

disabled unable to do something, such as behave or move in a certain way

disorder when something, such as the brain, is not working properly

heart attack when the heart suddenly stops working properly. This is very dangerous, and the person must receive medical help right away.

insulin chemical that controls how much sugar is in a person's blood

laboratory room where scientists use special equipment to do things such as blood tests or examine cells taken from patients

long-term for a long time. A long-term illness may remain for months or even years.

malignant type of growth caused by the disease cancer. A malignant tumor often gets worse and can spread, causing serious health problems.

mental disorder repeated ways of thinking or behaving in a person that makes him or her suffer and not always be able to live a normal life

metabolism process through which food is broken down in the body

obesity condition of being very overweight

starvation extreme hunger due to a lack of eating essential foods

stem cell cell that can renew itself or multiply, making new body tissue

support group people who gather together and talk because they share a common experience, such as an illness like diabetes

vaccinated when a "mock" germ has been put into the body. This gets the body to produce defenses in case the real, harmful germ invades.

vegetative state describes a patient with brain damage who is unaware of his or her surroundings

virus microscopic creature that feeds inside the cells of other creatures; viruses cause illnesses such as colds and AIDS

X-ray special type of photograph that shows the bones and organs inside the body

Find Out More

Books

Amos, Janine. *Going to the Hospital* (*Changes*). New York: Alphabet Soup, 2010.

DeGezelle, Terri. *Illness* (*The Real Deal*). Chicago: Heinemann Library, 2009.

Duckworth, Katie. *Health* (*Children's Rights*). Mankato, Minn.: Smart Apple Media, 2005.

Goulding, Sylvia. *Illness and Injury* (*Healthy Kids*). Vero Beach, Fla.: Rourke, 2005.

Levete, Sarah. *Health and Disease* (*Headline Issues*). Chicago: Heinemann Library, 2009.

Websites and organizations

The following organizations and websites can offer help, support, and information for you and your family:

www.kidshealth.com
Kids' Health is a website that gives information about how to keep healthy, different illnesses and conditions, what it's like visiting the hospital, and much more.

Children's Cancer Association
www.joyrx.org
Visit the Children's Cancer Association website to find out how this charity helps families dealing with cancer, and to read blogs by children battling with the disease.

Children's Cancer Research Fund
www.childrenscancer.org/stories-of-hope/kids-stories
Visit this website to read kids' stories about beating cancer.

Autism Speaks

www.autismspeaks.org

This website helps people with autism and their families stay up-to-date on the latest research and learn more about autism.

National Eating Disorders Association

www.nationaleatingdisorders.org

Visit this website for information on eating disorders, how to get help, and what you can do to help someone you know who has an eating disorder.

Children with Diabetes

www.childrenwithdiabetes.com

This website will help you and your family get in touch with other children with diabetes.

American Association of Caregiving Youth

www.aacy.org

The American Association of Caregiving Youth is a group supporting young caregivers in the United States. The website is packed with helpful information, advice, support, and recreational activities designed to give young caregivers time out. There are also forums where you can express your thoughts.

ADDitude

www.additudemag.com

This online magazine provides information about living with ADD, plus it provides forums, blogs, and links to additional resources.

About Our Kids

www.aboutourkids.org

This website is dedicated to the issue of how children are affected by mental health issues. See videos of other kids' experiences and find lots of information about mental health issues at this website.

Index